NOTES OF
PARAGUAY

Introduction to Paraguay Capital Markets

JORGE DANIEL "JD" USANDIVARAS

Archway Publishing books may be ordered through booksellers or by contacting:

Archway Publishing
1663 Liberty Drive
Bloomington, IN 47403
www.archwaypublishing.com
844-669-3957

Because of the dynamic nature of the Internet, any web addresses or links contained in this book may have changed since publication and may no longer be valid. The views expressed in this work are solely those of the author and do not necessarily reflect the views of the publisher, and the publisher hereby disclaims any responsibility for them.

Any people depicted in stock imagery provided by Getty Images are models, and such images are being used for illustrative purposes only.
Certain stock imagery © Getty Images.

As any publication of this nature, the information contained on these pages is considered to be up to date and verified, in addition, "The market commentary contained herein and should not be construed as investment advice or recommendations to buy or sell securities. The author disclaims liability for any profits or losses resulting from the use of information in this document."

ISBN: 978-1-6657-6904-4 (sc)
ISBN: 978-1-6657-6948-8 (hc)
ISBN: 978-1-6657-6905-1 (e)

Library of Congress Control Number: 2024924682

Print information available on the last page.

Archway Publishing rev. date: 02/18/2025

Table of Contents

CHAPTER

Paraguay as a Green and Sustainable Country

Paraguay has been poetically described by the Paraguayan novelist Roa Bastos as an 'island surrounded by land.' This vision of an 'island' evokes an image of green as the color that Paraguay has in abundance. The idea of being 'surrounded by land' is partially true, as its vast neighbors, Brazil and Argentina, seem as immense as oceans. However, one might be mistaken in thinking that Paraguay is landlocked, given that it lies between the Paraná and Paraguay rivers, which gives the country a central role in a very important waterway (hydrovia). It boasts the largest barge fleet in South America and the third largest in the world, after the United States and China. It has extensive access to the Guarani Aquifer, the largest freshwater reserve in the world. Paraguay is not exactly a dry land.

Since 2020, Paraguayan companies have been increasingly classifying their debt obligations as 'green' or 'sustainable' under international ESG standards, as most of the country's real economy does. Like many countries that have skipped the rudiments of industrialization, the so-called "import substitution," Paraguay is largely unscathed from chemical and metal pollution in its lands and waters and, becoming ever more important, has a 100% carbon-free electricity grid, capable of generating strong and sustainable economic development.

Power generation and distribution are useful ways to understand the country as a whole, its blessings, and its curses. The government is planning actions and policies to improve the country's electricity distribution system. This is reflected in the investment project of the National Electricity Administration (ANDE). The energy investment master plan projects an investment of $6.2 billion in key infrastructure, such as transmission, distribution, and energy generation, over 10 years (2021-2030). This investment was expected to average $620 million per year. However, at the time of writing this article, the execution has been much lower, with an annual average of only $300 million between 2021 and 2023.

From the Capital Markets Perspective

Paraguay incorporated the guidelines into its regulation for the issuance of bonds for Sustainable Development Goals (SDG). On March 5, 2020, the National Securities Commission (CNV), now the Superintendency of Securities, approved Resolution No. 9/20, which provides comprehensive legislation for "the securities market with new financial instruments that promote social and environmental issues," in line with the SDGs of the 2030 Agenda of the United Nations. The bonds issued under this resolution require standard certification from firms accredited under the Climate Bonds Initiative.

In turn, the Asunción Stock Exchange (BVA) signed an agreement in December 2020 with the SSE Initiative (Sustainable Stock Exchanges), the United Nations (UN) office, to adjust the issuance of Paraguay's green bonds to international standards. This is not the first agreement of this type, as in 2019, the Asunción Stock Exchange also signed an agreement with the UNEP FI (Financing Initiative of the United Nations Environment Program) and with the Sustainable Finance Table (MFS). This non-profit association seeks to lead Paraguay's financial sector towards economically sustainable parameters.

Beyond the legal framework led by the regulators and the Asuncion Exchange, it is in the minds and hearts of most Paraguayans that they should avoid the depletion of natural resources and maintain an ecological balance. Now, the onus is more on the business community to adopt good practices that can be "doing well by doing good."

Environmental Context

Sustainability or corporate social responsibility can be considered synonymous since both terms refer to the idea of maintaining something without affecting current or future generations. In other words, it is to avoid the depletion of natural resources and to maintain an ecological balance. Thus, these terms have come to encompass almost all business practices that can be classified as "doing well by doing good," becoming an overused label that has been replaced by a more meaningful term, "ESG."

ESG, as a definition for "Environmental, social and governance," is perhaps more accepted by capital market certifiers than the UN's DSG. It includes how a bond issuer manages relationships with employees, suppliers, customers, and the communities where it operates and deals with the standards set by the leadership of an issuer, its executive compensation, audits, internal controls, and shareholder rights.

Paraguay bonds have already met, through multiple certifications, the criteria of the type "ES = Environmental, Social." New opportunities are opening up within sustainable finance as a result of its clean and green energy (hydroelectric dams), legal efforts to avoid deforestation (however not fully met in practice), lack of large polluting industries, and no nuclear. Paraguay is itself, at a glance, "green and sustainable" and certifiable for market participants.

Paraguay as Environmental and Social (ES)

In December 2020, Banco Continental, a large local bank, launched its first ESG 144A bond in the market, becoming the first financial institution in the country to issue a sustainable bond in international markets for a value of $300 million, at a nominal rate of 2.75% and maturing in December 2025. The issue has a BB + rating (Fitch Ratings). The bank carried out the issuance in line with the Sustainable Development Goals established by the United Nations, which have been detailed in the [1]Framework of the sustainable bond and were[2] verified by Sustainalytics, a leading independent firm in research, rating, and analysis of corporate governance. It has been certified by the Climate Bonds Standard Board as a verification organization. Interestingly, the bonds were not available to Paraguayans (unless they had offshore accounts in US dollars), and it was a resounding success.

---

[1] Link to the 'framework' of the sustainable bond of Banco Continental:
https://www.bancontinental.com.py/Files/Banco%20Continental%20Sustainability%20Bond%20Framework November2020.pdf.

[2] Link to the Sustainalytics verification of the 'framework':
https://www.bancontinental.com.py/Files/Banco%20Continental%20Green%20Bond%20Framework%20Second%20 Party%20Opinion%20(1).pdf

There are significant precedents to the Continental bonds in the Paraguay financial industry: The Overseas Private Investment Corporation (OPIC), together with Citibank, signed an agreement for a loan to Banco Sudameris for $102 million over nine years under the 2x Initiative program to support the leadership and equity of women in American companies. This initiative seeks to support companies led by women that offer products or services that empower women internationally. This loan to the local bank is intended to help strengthen the long-term financing of SMEs in the country. Its main objective is to encourage the leadership and equity of Paraguayan women within the business and entrepreneurial sector.

In 2023, the Development Finance Agency (AFD), a second-tier bank, conducted the first issuance of Sustainable Bonds at the local level through the Asunción Stock Exchange. The issuance of the SDG Bonds was valued at $13 million (Gs. 100,000 million). It was a total success, with 100% of the planned amount placed in the first issuance. The securities are backed by the Public Treasury and have a minimum denomination of $137 (Gs. 1 million), with a 3-year term. The coupon interest rate was 7% per annum, with quarterly interest payments and capital amortization at maturity. The funds obtained from this first issuance will be allocated to finance housing programs, education, and the development of environmental projects.

Governance (G)

However, in terms of "governance," most experts signal that Paraguay has an important job to do, and even more so, taking into account that international rating agencies emphasize Paraguay in terms of "G" of Governance. Under most accepted Latin American standards, the term "governability" or good governance defines a set of processes and institutions through which power is exercised in a country and where it is determined to develop its economic and social resources. This is also referred to as the quality of the judiciary as an institution and government subject to the rule of law. The Paraguayan Congress is a very strong institution under any measure. However, Paraguay does not come up to the mark on the rule of law and the quality of its judiciary, although private enterprises have made a greater effort. Expanding the concept of 'Governance' to the business context and addressing individual company's leadership, executive compensation, audits, internal controls, and minority shareholders' rights, we note that many local businesses are properly run and could achieve SEG certifications.

Landmark Cases

Two important examples can be seen in Paraguay's short capital markets history. The first is the Velox Group case [3]. The Velox case led to a financial crisis with a widespread social impact. It was related to the Argentine default of 2002 and affected Paraguay and neighboring countries. Shareholders at the holding company level faced serious accusations by the courts from Paraguay, Uruguay, and Argentina.

In Paraguay, the group was made up of Banco Alemán Paraguayo, Financiera Parapití, Inversiones Guaraní (Investment funds), Inversiones Velox (brokerage house), Planning Financiero y Pensiones SA (trust company), and Santa Isabel ('*Stock*' supermarket chains). In Argentina, they maintained Banco Velox and a chain of supermarkets and, in Uruguay, Banco Montevideo, BM Fondos de Inversión, and Indumex. The holding also had operations in Brazil, Chile, and Peru. Velox owners were accused of irregular management and the decapitalization of the financial institution in Uruguay; in Argentina, the operations of Banco Velox were suspended for the same reason, and in Paraguay, they were accused of fraudulent dealings with Banco Alemán.

---

[3] Link to the ABC Digital article: https://www.abc.com.py/edicion-impresa/economia/un-terremoto-sacude-al-grupo-velox-en-toda-la-region-652559.html

More than 20 years later, after many comings and goings, judicial processes, escapes, and extraditions, there is still no resolution to the case. Investors and savers continue to fight to recover some of their money. Investor mistrust in the entire asset management industry is still felt to this day.

Another important case brought before the Paraguay judiciary is known as "Electrofácil," after the company that had a successful listing in the local market (2013), as well as in the international market (2014). It was the first entirely Paraguayan company to be listed on the London Junior Exchange[4]. Allegedly, in 2015, before finalizing the sale of the company, its executives faked the value of its operations, increasing the valuation. Currently, former shareholders and executives are accused by the buyers of fraud and the production of false documents, as well as charges of money laundering.

Several years after the start of the legal cases against Electrofácil, the process moves slowly. The pace of the case is relevant for the different rating agencies, as it signals the vulnerability of the country's justice system, marking Paraguay and its judiciary as non-compliant with the Governance criterion of "ESG."

Macroeconomic Data

Population and GDP Per Capita

Paraguay, located in the heart of South America, has an area of 406,752 km² (157,048 mi²). It is sparsely populated and ranks 224th in the world population table out of 250 countries. According to data from the latest National Census conducted by the National Institute of Statistics (INE), in 2022, the population was 6,109,903 inhabitants, of which 50.05% or 3,057,674 are men and 49.95% or 3,052,229 are women.

---

[4] http://acfequityresearch.com/wp-content/uploads/2015/10/LATS-GX-Investment-Summary-Plus-FINAL-08012015.pdf.pdf

Country	Land Area (km²)	Population Density (km²)
Finland	336,884	16
Poland	313,931	120
Oman	309,980	15
Vietnam	331,340	298
Ivory Coast	322,462	90
Malaysia	330,621	104
Republic of Congo	342,000	18
Germany	357,581	233
Japan	377,930	326
Norway	385,207	14
Zimbabwe	390,757	43
Paraguay	**406,752**	**15**

Land Area & Population Density (km²) as of 2023.
Source: Own elaboration with data from the United Nations.

Despite its small population, largely concentrated in three cities, when Paraguay is compared to the other countries, it is relatively large: 406,752 km² (157,047 mi²) or larger than Germany, Japan, Norway, and Poland. However, its population density of 15 inhabitants per km² makes the country one of the least inhabited on the list. As an example, Vietnam, with a smaller land area than Paraguay, has a population density of 298 inhabitants per km².

Continuing with our analysis, it can be seen that the Paraguayan economy stands out as one of the smallest within a regional and global context. According to estimates from the Central Bank of Paraguay, the country's GDP in 2023 reached $43 billion, with a GDP per capita of $5,693. When comparing these results with data from other countries provided by the World Bank, it is evident that Paraguay holds a relatively modest position in terms of economic size.

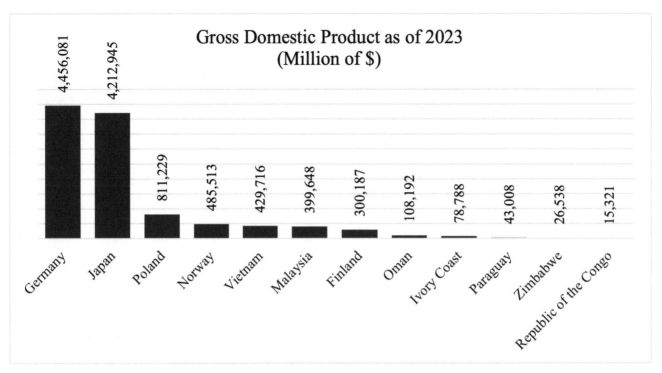

Comparative Gross Domestic Product (GDP) as of 2023.
Source: Own elaboration with data from the World Bank and Central Bank of Paraguay.

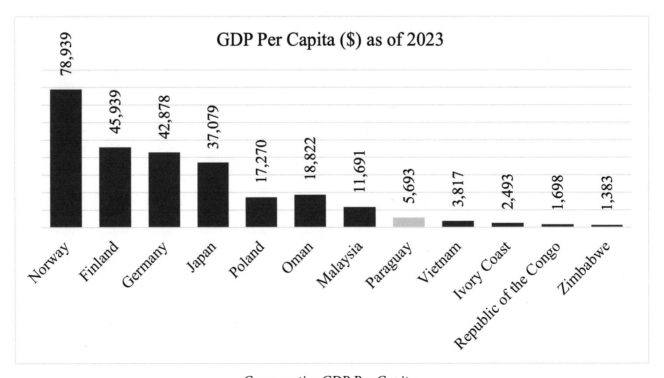

Comparative GDP Per Capita.
Source: Own elaboration with data from the World Bank and Central Bank of Paraguay.

Analyzing the graphs above, we note that Germany is one of the countries with the highest GDP, followed by Japan. With further analysis, we note that the countries with a GDP of less than $1,000 billion are Poland, Norway, Vietnam, Malaysia, Finland and Oman. The countries with a GDP of less than $100 million are the

Ivory Coast, Paraguay, Zimbabwe, and the Republic of the Congo. On a GDP Per Capita basis, Paraguay is $5,647. This is in stark comparison to wealthy Norway, which also has a low population density but a high GDP.

According to statistics from the National Institute of Statistics, in 2022, half of the population was 29 years old or younger. Paraguay is also a country of emigration, which is largely explained by its low GDP. According to data published by the International Organization for Migration (IOM), an agency associated with the United Nations, in 2020, a total of 867,511 Paraguayans were living abroad for work and settlement purposes. The geographical distribution of these emigrants shows a majority concentration in Argentina, followed by Spain and Brazil, in that order.

Paraguay Historical Data and Projections

A significant portion of Paraguay's economy relies on agriculture and livestock, making climatic conditions a crucial factor. A good year in these sectors decisively contributes to Paraguay closing with positive results. According to data from the Central Bank of Paraguay (BCP), the country's GDP grew by 3.6% in 2018. For 2019, initial estimates were for 4% growth. However, as the year progressed, expectations diminished, and the economy ultimately grew by 3.5%.

By the end of 2020, the Central Bank of Paraguay projected a GDP contraction of -1.0% as a result of the persistent effects of the COVID-19 pandemic and lower agricultural production. Nevertheless, Paraguay stood out in the region as the most resilient economy during the pandemic, experiencing the smallest contraction among all the countries in the region[5]. For 2021, the preliminary economic growth was estimated at 5%. However, the GDP ultimately recorded a growth of 4.2%. This slowdown compared to the initial expectations was largely due to climatic factors, with drought significantly affecting the last quarter of the year and the subsequent period. The effects of the drought continued to be felt during the first months of 2022. Added to this were the economic repercussions of the war between Russia and Ukraine, resulting in minimal GDP growth, which ultimately increased by just 0.1%.

In 2023, Paraguay closed the year with solid economic growth, according to the Monetary Policy Report (IpoM) published by the Central Bank of Paraguay. The report indicates that accumulated GDP growth was 4.7%, driven primarily by agriculture, livestock, manufacturing, electricity generation, and the services sector. The Economic Commission for Latin America and the Caribbean (ECLAC) ranked Paraguay as the third fastest-growing economy in the region in 2023.

At the time of writing this article, the Central Bank of Paraguay indicated that GDP growth estimates for 2024 are 3.8%, driven primarily by the manufacturing, construction, energy generation, commerce, and services sectors.

---

[5] Link to the MarketData article: https://marketdata.com.py/noticias/bm-confirma-a-paraguay-como-el-pais-con-menor-caida-economica-en-la-region-en-2020-y-eleva-a-35-la-proyeccion-2021-47690/

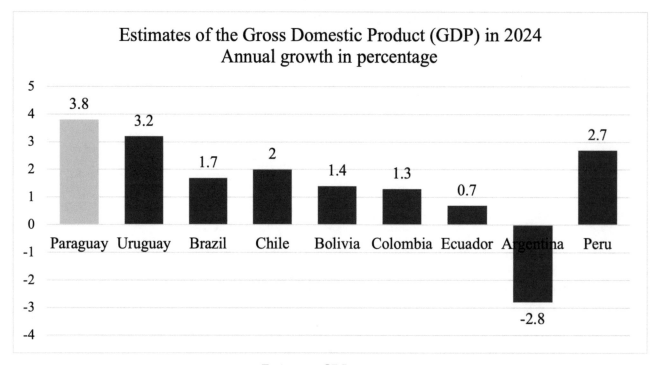

Estimates GDP in 2024.
Source: Own elaboration with data from the World Bank.

Paraguay's Inflation

In 2020, Paraguay registered inflation of 2.2%, the lowest since the records started under the current BCP methodology in 2009. This is lower than the 2.8% registered in 2019, which reflected the decline in economic activity over a long period. By 2021, inflation climbed to 6.8%. Several factors contributed to this increase, including rising international prices, supply chain issues, climatic factors, and domestic demand, among others.

The rise in prices continued through 2022, with inflation climbing even higher to 8.1%, a figure that surpassed initial expectations and was one of the highest in the past decade for the country. In 2023, accumulated inflation significantly decreased to 3.8%. This decline was due to a combination of factors, including better stability in international prices, the normalization of supply chains, and the monetary policies of the Central Bank of Paraguay, which helped contain inflation. At the time of writing this Note, the Central Bank of Paraguay projects that inflation in 2024 will reach 4%.

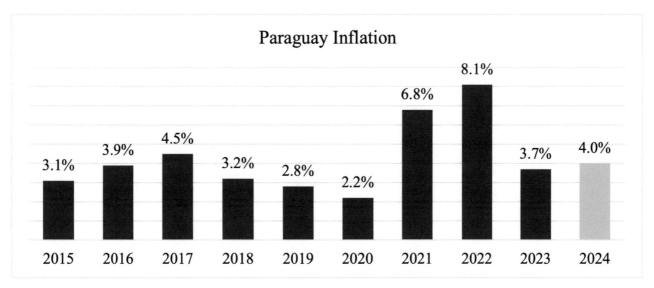

Historical Paraguay Inflation.
Source: Own elaboration with data from the Central Bank of Paraguay.

Paraguay's Exchange Rate

In December 2023, the wholesale reference price of the Central Bank of Paraguay in US dollars closed at $1/Gs. 7,263.59 in the purchase and $1/Gs. 7,283.62 for sale. According to BCP records, the highest peak of the year was reached on November 1st, when it stood at ($1/Gs. 7,474.57). The dollar appreciated by 0.07% compared to January 2023 ($1/Gs. 7,269.13) and depreciated by 0.24% compared to November 30th ($1/Gs. 7,419.12). Meanwhile, the Central Bank of Paraguay (reported sales - from January to December 2023) amounting to $1,129.58 million to ease the demand for dollars. Total Net International Reserves at the end of December 2023 amounted to $10,196.8 million, higher than the $9,825.0 million recorded the previous year.

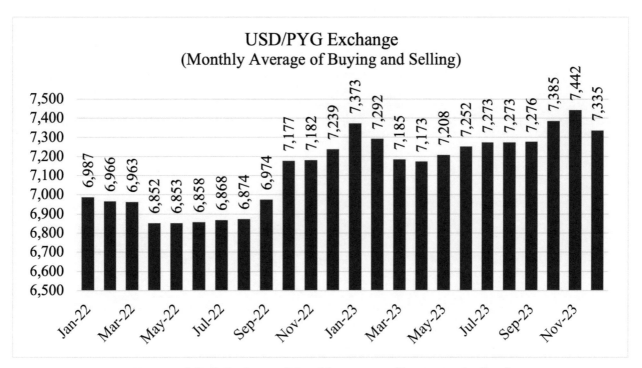

Historical Gs/$ Exchange (Monthly average of buying and selling).
Source: Own elaboration with data from the Central Bank of Paraguay.

Risk, Returns, Ratings, Terms, and Liquidity.

A Brief History of Paraguay Capital Markets

**Stock Exchange and Products of Asunción (BVPASA)
– Now, Asunción Stock Exchange (BVA)**

© Bolsa de Valores Asunción.
Opening Session of the Asunción Commodity and Stock Exchange.
Source: Book 114 years CNCSP.

Towards the end of the 1970s, all large South American countries, such as Brazil, Argentina, Peru, Colombia, and Chile, boasted thriving stock markets with up to 100 years of history. In 1977, Paraguay's[6] National Chamber of Commerce and Services founded the first, and to date, only Stock & Commodity Exchange in the country, the "*Bolsa de Valores y Productos de Asunción S.A.*" or (BVPASA).

Historians still argue the reasons BVPASA didn't operate fully during the government of General Stroessner. Some mentioned the prevailing political regime's restrictions, others the lack of a free market economy, incomplete legal framework, and low levels of knowledge about an open exchange by both entrepreneurs and the investor public. The fact is that there were minimal transactions during the 70s and 80s, and eventually, the market ceased negotiations.

Fast forward to 1991, with a new democratic political regime, the Paraguay Congress enacted Act No. 94/91, a new legal framework for the Securities Market. The local regulator, the Superintendency of Securities, was also created. About a year later, the exchange restarted operations that continue and expand to this day, helped by sustained GDP growth. Bond buying presented an alternative to the only locally available savings method, bank-issued *Certificado de Depósito de Ahorro* (CDAs). At the time of writing this Note, a financial instrument regulated by the Central Bank of Paraguay, CDAs remain the most common savings instrument for both individuals and corporations. As of December 2023, with a total of around $8.0 billion. CDAs offer an average yield of 8.33% for the local currency and 5.82% for the US dollar for terms exceeding 365 days.

In 2021, the Asunción Stock Exchange and Products (BVPASA, for its Spanish acronym) implemented a strategy to renew its corporate image. As part of this initiative, the institution adopted a new denomination, officially changing its name to "Asunción Stock Exchange" with the acronym "BVA." Throughout the text, we will delve into the details of this new branding.

1990s, a New Era for the Paraguayan Stock Market.

BVA officially resumed its trading sessions in October 1993, this time under the supervision of the newly created National Securities Commission (CNV), now known as the Superintendency of Securities. Fixed-income instruments, in various forms of bonds, quickly became the most commonly traded regulated securities in Paraguay under the CNV at that time. Like most Latin American economies, private companies are family-owned and are not listed despite tax incentives (see Act No. 548/95[7]). Therefore, although they are very valuable instruments, equity stock volume is unimportant for the Asuncion exchange.

When the Stock Market reopened, Paraguay went through a deep economic recession in 1995[8], following the introduction of democracy, financial liberalization, the lack of adequate control and supervision regimes, widespread corruption, and the omission of regulations. Basic legal provisions and the opportunity to make large profits in the short term led to the start-up of many banks and finance companies, from 88 entities at the end of 1988 to 147 at the beginning of 1995. From that year on, the Central Bank made interventions in

---

[6] The NATIONAL CHAMBER OF COMMERCE AND SERVICES OF PARAGUAY is a non-profit entity, founded on May 25, 1898. Through more than 110 years of history it has devoted its efforts to two specific areas: capital markets and alternative conflict resolution methods. The Chamber contributed to the creation of the Asunción Stock and Commodities Exchange and the Paraguayan Arbitration and Mediation Center.

[7] https://www.bacn.gov.py/leyes-paraguayas/2446/ley-n-548-sobre-retasacion-y-regularizacion-extraordinaria-de-bienes-de-empresas

[8] https://www.elibrary.imf.org/view/IMF087/10077-9789996760105/10077-9789996760105/ch03.xml?language=en&redirect=true&redirect=true

several financial institutions due to serious liquidity problems, which ended in the cessation of operations of the audited entities after demonstrating that their assets were inflated or did not exist, while their liabilities were grossly underestimated. Large national banks and financial institutions went bankrupt, such as Bancopar and General, Bancosur, Banco Mercantil, Banco Unión, and Banco de Inversiones del Paraguay, among others, and financial institutions such as Urundey, Sauce, Vanguardia, and Sur de Finanzas, etc., because of the financial crisis, as well as because of the Tequila Effect[9], which was a financial crisis that occurred in Mexico in the same year and with great repercussions in Latin America. The total cost of the crisis was estimated to be between 10% and 12% of the Gross Domestic Product (GDP). Congress enacted Organic Act No. 489/1995[10], modernizing the Central Bank of Paraguay, and Act No. 797/95[11] for financial stabilization and reactivation.

During the Paraguay version of the Tequila Crisis, the Paraguay Bolsa continued its work of consolidating its infrastructure, educating its officers, and adding market participants. Over the years, a few bills were created to develop the local markets:

- In 1995:
  Act No. 548/95 on Revaluation and Regularization of Business Assets.

- In 1996:
  Act No. 921/96 Regulation of Trusts and Trustees,
  Act No. 1017/96 to authorize the first issuance of Paraguay treasury bonds.

- 1997:
  Act No. 1036/97 regulates securitizations.
  Act No. 1056/97 regulates Credit Rating companies and,
  Act No. 1163/97 regulates the establishment of commodity exchanges.

- In 1998:
  Act No. 1284/98, the new Securities Market Act

By 2006, BVA was expanding and moved its offices within the Chamber of Commerce and Services of Paraguay to its own building in Asuncion Downtown's 15 de Agosto Street.

Early in this century, BVA entered into agreements with the Argentine Rosario Futures Exchange (ROFEX) to incorporate its electronic exchange platform. By 2010, BVA implemented the Electronic Trading System (SEN), which, over the years, has adapted and evolved and connected with other Stock Exchanges worldwide. In 2012, BVA signed a contract with Argentina Clearing S.A. to develop a trading platform for the Guaraní-Dollar currency futures market that began operations in 2013. By 2015, the trading platform incorporated systems for securities "Repurchase Operations" or "REPOS," which, to date, are the most actively traded contracts on BVA, or 70.8% of its entire operations.

---

[9] https://economipedia.com/definiciones/crisis-tequila.html

[10] https://www.mic.gov.py/mic/w/comercio/dgcs/pdf/6_Servicios_Financieros/LEY_N_489-95_organica_BCP.pdf

[11] https://www.bacn.gov.py/leyes-paraguayas/2451/estabilizacion-y-reactivacion-financiera

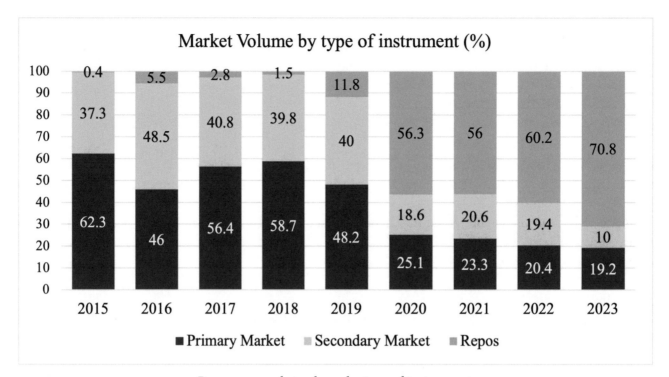

Market Volume by type of instrument (%)

Paraguay market volume by type of instrument.
Source: Own elaboration with data from the Superintendency of Securities.

2017 saw a complete revamp of the domestic securities regulations and the birth of Verbank Securities Casa de Bolsa S.A., an affiliate of Verbank Holdings, the first American broker-dealer to have a seat on the Exchange. By July 2017, the Superintendency of Securities presented a bill to Congress, which in June 2018 was enacted as Congressional Act No. 5810/17[12], superseding virtually all previous Acts and, for the first time, allowing domestic broker-dealers to trade international securities.

The new Act expands and updates numerous established points in Paraguay and includes new provisions to facilitate the country's stock market development, granting access to large issuers and mid-sized companies. We can definitely say that Act No. 5810/17, continually in force in Paraguay together with the body of regulations enacted by the Superintendency of Securities in Resolutions No. 1 to 30/21,[13] gave new life to the local securities markets and asset managers and set the groundwork for its current and future expansion.

In 2018, BVA signed a cooperation agreement with CBONDS to provide more information to the market and reach new investors. With this agreement, information about the issuers registered with BVA can be searched through the CBONDS platform. That same year, the Bolsa enabled the Commodities Exchange in Paraguay to offer a trading platform for transactions in the local agricultural sector, allowing the registration of bilateral contracts of cattle, soybeans, corn, wheat, and rice. However, at the time of writing this Note, the Paraguayan Commodity Exchange is on pause due to a lack of market demand.

In 2019, the BVA ended the dematerialization of bonds and shares by registering the first Paraguayan company to issue its own electronic shares. That same year, the BVA launched its price viewer, providing more information, volume charts, and real-time bids. To date, 268 issuers are registered in the Electronic Trading System, of which 100 are Publicly Traded Corporations (Sociedad Anónima Emisora de Capital Abierto) and

---

[12] https://www.cnv.gov.py/normativas/leyes/ley_no_5810_17.pdf

[13] https://www.cnv.gov.py/normativas/resoluciones/Res_CG_30_Nuevo_RGMV_aut.pdf

96 are Private Corporations (Sociedad Anónima Emisora). In 2023 alone, 19 issuers were registered, of which 12 belong to Private Corporations and 5 to Publicly Traded Corporations. The remaining 2 registrations correspond to a Cooperative and a Multilateral Organization.

By 2020, after 14 years of continuous operations, the building on Calle 15 de Agosto became the Stock Exchange's back office. The Exchange moved to a new, modern building located in Asuncion's modern corporate center, about nine kilometers east of downtown, in Villa Morra. The Bolsa also signed the Letter of Commitment with the association to the Sustainable Stock Exchange (SSE) initiative and implemented the 'BVPASA Study Center' to provide high-quality training services to investors, issuers, and the general public.

© *Bolsa de Valores Asunción.*
The new and current BVPASA building on Villa Morra.
Source: Own elaboration with data from Diary ABC Color.

In April 2021, after 14 years, BVA renewed its directors and appointed a new president, Mr. Eduardo Borgognon Montero, who succeeds Rodrigo Callizo at the helm. The president of the exchange is a public accountant and finance director of a multinational metallurgical industry (CIE).

The achievements at BVA during Rodrigo Callizo's tenure as president include:

- Cooperation agreement with ROFEX, 2007.
- Implementation of the Electronic Trading System (SEN), 2010.
- Dematerialization of Fixed Income Bonds, 2010.
- Implementation of Repo Operations, 2015.

- Launch of Gs/$ Futures contracts, 2017.
- Launch of the Product Exchange, 2017.
- Issuance of the first dematerialized shares, 2019.
- Signing a letter of commitment with the SSE on the issuance of ODS bonds, 2020.
- The historic record of volume traded reached $1,985 million in 2020.

The new image of the Asunción Stock Exchange: BVA

BVA, in a re-branding process, changed its name in the market and is now BVA. In this way, the BVA seeks to highlight, with a new face, the achievements of recent years and the projects to come.

Eduardo Borgognon, president of the BVA, pointed out in an interview that they seek to generate a new image before the market and society. Likewise, he indicated that the company will bet heavily on the dissemination of relevant information, both for investors and potential issuers. *"The idea is to tell the experiences of the issuers and how the foray into the stock market to finance themselves benefited their companies. The idea is to generate a story to promote emissions through the BVA, and in this sense, information for companies will be essential in different ways,"* Eduardo noted. In this way, they will seek to show companies the benefits of the capital market in terms of the possibilities of financing their projects.

©Bolsa de Valores Asunción.
Before and after the re-branding process.

Stock market evolution, growth, and development.

After implementing the Electronic Trading System (SEN) in the stock market, the Paraguayan exchange has evolved significantly. By the end of 2023, the BVA reported a total of 23 registered brokerage firms, with six new additions during that year alone. In terms of trading on the BVA (Fixed Income, Equities, Repos, FX Derivatives), the total volume reached $5.083 billion, representing 14% of Paraguay's GDP and marking an 83% increase compared to 2022. There has been rapid growth in Mutual Funds and Investment Funds. By the end of 2023, the total assets of both amounted to $1.527 billion, with 26 Mutual Funds and 15 Investment Funds authorized to operate. Although the trading volume is still small compared to neighboring countries in the region, the growth of this sector in Paraguay and the introduction of simple yet effective new regulations indicate that it will expand geometrically.

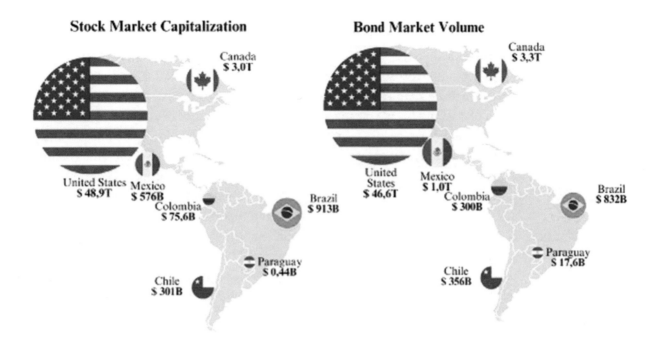

Stock Market Capitalization

Canada
$ 3,0T

United States
$ 48,9T

Mexico
$ 576B

Colombia
$ 75,6B

Brazil
$ 913B

Paraguay
$ 0,44B

Chile
$ 301B

Bond Market Volume

Canada
$ 3,3T

United
States
$ 46,6T

Mexico
$ 1,0T

Colombia
$ 300B

Brazil
$ 832B

Paraguay
$ 17,6B

Chile
$ 356B

Global stock market comparison.
Sources: Bank for International Settlements (BIS); World Exchange Federation (WFE).

It is worth mentioning that the expansion of the markets requires a great deal of education, not only by the market participants but also for the general investor public. The Superintendency of Securities, BVA, and a growing number of privately led efforts continue developing and promoting classes and seminars about the exchange markets in Paraguay.

National Securities Comission (Comisión Nacional de Valores or "CNV").

Brief Historical Review.

The Superintendency of Securities is the regulatory body of the Paraguayan securities market. In 1991, following the enactment of Law No. 94/91, the National Securities Commission (CNV) was established, which is now known as the Superintendency of Securities. This law provided the necessary legal framework for the initiation, development, and strengthening of stock market operations.

In 1998, the new Securities Market Act, Act No. 1284/98, granted autonomy to the Superintendency of Securities as the competent authority in matters of the securities market, with the power to apply sanctions and corrective measures to any activity related to any local securities markets.

The Superintendency of Securities has worked to dictate and apply new regulations to develop the market and its technological and human infrastructure throughout its existence. It has achieved greater control effectiveness than others. *"The CNV establishes the rules of the game and acts as an impartial arbitrator, allowing the fair and transparent economic activity to the various market agents,"* said the then President, Mr. Jorge Luis Schreiner Marengo, who encouraged and looked optimistically at the markets seeking to turn it into the main engine of the national economy. Other landmark achievements of his tenure are:

- In 2004, simplification of the registration process for bonds with common guarantee after the enactment of Act No. 2421 on Fiscal Adequacy[14].
- In 2005, bond issuance through trusts. This constitutes a challenge for the CNV in terms of regulation and supervision since it involves two regulatory areas, the fiduciary and the stock market, and its success requires adequate inter-institutional coordination between the CNV and the BCP.
- In the market, these constitute an interesting alternative for the investment of financial resources due to the diversification of risk and the access to stock exchange instruments by small investors.
- In 2008, banks participated in the securities market in the issuance of subordinated bonds and preferred shares, instruments characterized by their long duration and the absence of investor guarantees.
- In 2009, Act No. 3899 was enacted, which regulates the operation of Risk Rating Societies, thus completing the institutional scheme required for investor decision-making.
- In 2012, a relevant stock market event after the approval and incursion of the Ministry of Finance as an issuer of National Treasury bonds through the Asunción Stock Exchange.
- In 2013, Act No. 4919/13 was enacted, authorizing the Central Bank of Paraguay (BCP) to transfer a property for consideration in favor of the National Securities Commission (CNV) that will be used for the headquarters of the institution. It is expected that by 2015, after preparing the premises, the CNV will operate from its own premises after more than almost 20 years of institutional life. Also, in 2013, after 10 years as head of the institution, President Jorge Luis Schreiner Marengo resigned to join the private sector. The newly designated President is Mr. Fernando A. Escobar E.
- In 2015, the enactment of the new Act No. 5452 regulating Equity Investment Funds provided the market with a new legal framework more adapted to its needs to develop this type of instrument. Res. CNV No. 10E / 15 was also issued, which approves the Negotiation Regulations for Repo Transactions through the Electronic Trading System.
- In 2017, the promulgation of the new Securities Market Act No. 5810 replaced the previous Act No. 1284/98. This was to achieve an updated and comprehensive regulation of everything related to the public offering of securities and the agents that interact in said market.
- In 2018, the new president of the CNV, Mr. Joshua Abreu Boss, was appointed by the President of the Republic, Mr. Mario Abdo Benítez. In that same year, efforts in financial education also increased, highlighting the training provided by the entity in World Investor Week, in which more than 800 people participated, including university students, professionals in the area, and representatives of the private sector and civil society.
- In 2019, the General Securities Market Regulation was prepared, regulating Act No. 5810/17 of the Securities Market. Points that stand out in the new regulation include:
  - Prohibition of cash settlement of stock market operations.
  - Simplification of documentary requirements for registration.
  - Facilities for SME access to the stock market.
  - Application of the financial information standards prepared by the Council of Public Accountants of Paraguay.
  - Authorization to carry out international operations with securities not registered with the CNV.

In September 2023, the law "Creating the Superintendency of Securities to Replace the National Securities Commission and Granting it Greater Powers" was enacted. The new institution replaced the CNV as the authority responsible for regulating and supervising the securities market in Paraguay. Although it is part of

---

[14] http://www.oas.org/juridico/spanish/mesicic3_pry_ley2421.pdf

the Central Bank of Paraguay, the Superintendency of Securities has the autonomy to carry out its functions independently.

Unlike the CNV, the Superintendency has an expanded scope, allowing it to exercise stricter and more detailed market supervision, as well as the ability to issue regulations, impose sanctions, and conduct more rigorous audits to ensure transparency and security in the financial system. This modernization of the regulatory framework aims to align the supervision of the securities market with international standards, ensuring a more robust and reliable environment for investors.

Some of the functions of the Superintendency of Securities are:

- Supervise and inspect activities in the securities market as established by law and resolutions of the Central Bank of Paraguay.
- Monitor and ensure compliance with the Securities Market Law and its regulations.
- Ensure proper price formation in the markets and facilitate the dissemination of information to protect investors.
- Oversee and control individuals and entities operating in the securities market.
- Maintain the public registry of the securities market.
- Impose sanctions for violations of market regulations.
- Regulate and supervise the work of external auditors and suspend or cancel public offerings in case of irregularities.
- Inspect supervised individuals or entities and require the submission of truthful and timely financial information.

Current President of the Superintendency of Securities.

Joshua Daniel Abreu Boss and the New Generation.

With seven years as a portfolio manager at the Reserves Administration Department (DAR) of the Central Bank of Paraguay, an MBA from the University of Oxford, and a bachelor's degree awarded with a Gold Medal as the best student of the year in Finance at Roberts University Tulsa OK, Mr. Abreu is part of a new generation of public servants. In 2018, he was appointed president of the National Securities Commission (CNV), and following the creation of the Superintendency of Securities, the President of the Republic, Santiago Peña, appointed him as the superintendent of the new entity. At the time, Abreu expressed a strong desire to "*offer each Paraguayan opportunities to obtain capital to create their own business.*" He wanted citizens to have access to capital for the development of their own companies to create and generate work. "*It is important to understand that through the Stock Market, you can raise capital from abroad, and a lot of capital from abroad is wanting to invest in Paraguay,*" he said to the local newspapers at the time.[15]

Opening the market to Paraguayans to access securities from abroad and foreigners to access Paraguay securities is already a landmark of Mr. Abreus' administration. Given his young age, knowledge, and enthusiasm, it is expected that he will oversee the expansion and internationalization of the Paraguay securities markets.

---

[15] https://www.ultimahora.com/joshua-abreu-quiero-ser-parte-del-desarrollo-nuestro-pais-n2708490.html

Securities Depository of Paraguay S.A. (CAVAPY)

On September 20, 2022, the National Securities Commission officially registered Caja de Valores del Paraguay S.A. (CAVAPY) as a supervised entity under certificate No. 99. CAVAPY was established with the aim of aligning the Paraguayan capital market with international market structures, ensuring its modernization and competitiveness. At that time, CAVAPY's president, René Ruíz Díaz, stated, «Our country is facing a unique opportunity to advance on a path of long-term growth, and for that, the existence of a securities depository is essential. CAVAPY will be a key driver in facilitating and accelerating the arrival of capital to our market.

Caja de Valores is the specialized entity responsible for managing capital market operations. It operates as a custodian, clearinghouse, settlement, and payment entity for transactions conducted by various market participants, both in exchange-traded and over-the-counter operations. The primary role of Caja de Valores is to provide market participants, whether domestic or international, with peace of mind and security that their investments are being managed solidly.

CAVAPY offers a wide range of services that meet international standards, providing agile and secure solutions for investors. The company's shareholders include Banco Continental, Cadiem Casa de Bolsa, Investor Casa de Bolsa, and Puente Casa de Bolsa, all holding equal shares. At the time of writing this Note, the board of directors consists of Álvaro Acosta (president), Antonio Cejuela (vice-president), César Paredes (director), and René Ruíz Díaz (director).

CAVAPY offers the following key services:

- Securities Custody: Includes securities immobilization, dematerialization, and related registry services.
- Corporate Events: Manages maturity notifications, T0 collections, direct payments to investors or depositors, issuance of payment receipts, and information services.
- Clearing and Settlement: Manages OTC purchase/sale registrations, record updates, clearing and settlement of transactions, and information services.
- Certificates: Issues certificates upon maturity of securities, accredits ownership for the exercise of rights, and offers additional services such as CCN and information certification.

In June 2023, CAVAPY began its activities with the admission of four depositors. In September, the first physical securities were deposited for the exclusive custody service of physical securities, and their ownership was registered in the system and linked to the respective titleholder accounts.

In December, the managed custody service for physical securities was activated. This service includes the safekeeping of physical securities in the vault, registration of ownership in the system with the corresponding titleholder accounts, and the management of interest and amortization collections and payments for each depositor. CAVAPY ended 2023 with 644 titleholders and 472 titleholder accounts registered and active in the IT system. In December 2023, the nominal amount of securities under CAVAPY's custody closed at $113 million, reflecting a 29.5% growth in volume compared to the previous month and an 81.21% growth in volume compared to the close of the first operational month, resulting in an annual average growth of 22.5%.

As of December 31, 2023, the total custody was composed of 80% exclusive custody of securities, with 78% corresponding to savings certificates and 2% to physical shares, while the managed custody operation ended with 18% corresponding to savings certificates and the remaining 2% corresponding to the registration of CAVAPY's book-entry shares.

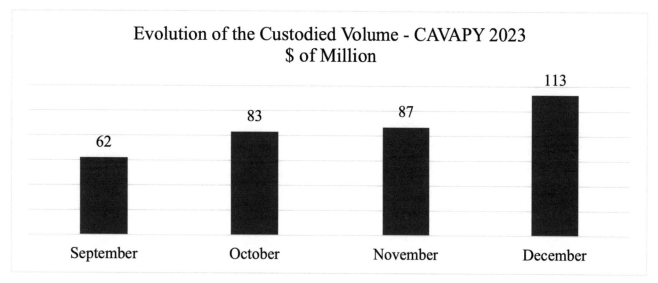

Paraguay Evolution of the custodied volume.
Source: Own elaboration with data from the Securities Depository of Paraguay.

Paraguay's debut in the international sovereign bond market.

In January 2013, under the government of Federico Franco, Paraguay made its debut in the international sovereign bond market with the launch of its first international bond with CITIGROUP as 'Global Coordinator' and BofA Merril Lynch as 'Joint Book-Runners.' The value of the issue was $500 million over 10 years, maturing in January 2023 at a nominal rate of 4.625%.

Paraguay, through the Ministry of Finance at that time, Mr. Manuel Ferreira Brusquetti, achieved resounding success in its first bond placement in the international market. The issuance of this bond set a precedent for the regional market because Paraguay, in a first-time issue, achieved the lowest rate of sovereign bonds and managed to place itself on the international radars of the financial world. At the end of 2012, the Bolivian government had also placed a sovereign bond worth $500 million at a rate of 4.8%, higher than that of Paraguay.

The great interest of investors in Paraguay was demonstrated by the oversubscribed demand of more than 11 times the nominal value. According to data, the demand reached $5,573 million compared to $500 million.

From 2013 to 2023, Paraguay has issued 12 sovereign bonds in the international market, with maturities currently ranging from 2026 to 2050. The 2023 bond has already been retired from circulation.

Paraguay Sovereign Bonds					
	Issue Date	Maturity Date	Amount (US$)	Nominal Rate (%)	Duration (Years)
Sovereign Bond 2023	25/1/13	25/1/23	450,494,000	4.625	10
Sovereign Bond 2044	11/8/14	11/8/44	1,000,000,000	6.10	30
Sovereign Bond 2026	23/3/16	15/4/26	600,000,000	5.00	10
Sovereign Bond 2027	22/3/17	27/3/27	500,000,000	4.70	10
Sovereign Bond 2048	8/3/18	13/3/48	530,000,000	5.60	30
Sovereign Bond 2050	4/2/19	30/3/50	1,175,858,000	5.40	31
Sovereign Bond 2031	23/4/20	28/4/31	1,000,000,000	4.95	11
Sovereign Bond 2033	20/1/21	29/1/33	600,000,000	2.739	11
Sovereign Bond 2033_2	20/1/22	28/6/33	500,600,000	3.849	10
Sovereign Bond 2033_3	28/6/23	21/8/33	500,000,000	5.850	10

Paraguay Sovereign Bonds.
Source: Own elaboration with data from the Ministry of Economy.

In 2015, the reopening of the 2023 Bond was carried out for a value of $280 million at a cutoff rate of 4.15%. In 2020, a reopening of the 2050 Bond was carried out for a value of $450 million at a cutoff rate of 4.45%. In 2021, the reopening of the 2050 Bond was carried out for a value of $225.8 million at a cutoff rate of 4.089%, along with a buyback of the 2023 Bond for $329.506 million. In 2022, the buyback of the 2023 Bond was carried out for $212.9 million and of the 2026 Bond for $72.9 million. In 2023, a buyback of the 2026 Bond was carried out for $70.264 million.

Corporate Titles in Paraguay.

Local Market and International Market.

By the end of 2023, 48 issuing companies traded bonds in the Electronic Trading System, with a total of 161 bonds, 22 subordinated bonds, 18 financial bonds, and three Short-Term Stock Exchange Bonds. On the equity side, during the same period, the BVA recorded 41 issuances of book-entry shares from five issuers. Additionally, no futures contracts were registered throughout that period.

Currently, nine corporate bonds from the following Paraguayan companies are trading on the international market: One bond from Banco Continental with a nominal rate of 2.75% and maturing in December 2025; One bond from Frigorifico Concepción with a nominal rate of 7.70% and maturing in July 2028; Six bonds from Millicom International Cellular (TIGO) with nominal rates of 6.00%, 6.625%, 5.125%, 6.25%, 4.5%, and 7.375%, and maturities in March 2025, October 2026, January 2028, March 2029, April 2031, and April 2032. Additionally, one bond from Telefónica Celular del Paraguay is listed with a nominal rate of 5.88% and maturing in April 2027. There are also listed bonds for public works with guarantees from governmental agencies, such as Routes 2 and 7 Finance LLC, maturing in September 2036, and Bioceanico (with sovereign guarantee), maturing in June 2034. As of today, there are no shares of Paraguayan companies trading on the international market.

As of August 31, 2024, there are 268 issuers registered in the Electronic Trading System. Of this total, 92 issuers have active bond registrations, and 21 issuers have registered shares. In terms of managed funds authorized to operate, there are 26 Mutual Funds, 15 Investment Funds, and 12 Investment Fund Management Companies. Paraguay has a single stock exchange: the Bolsa de Valores de Asunción (BVA). Currently, the market includes 24 authorized brokerage houses, approximately 64 stockbrokers, and 10 operators authorized to trade futures contracts.

Since 1993, the Paraguayan stock market has grown steadily, setting records in trading volume. In 2023, the stock market recorded an 83% increase compared to the total traded at the end of 2022. It is worth noting that Repo transactions in 2023 represented 70.8% of the total traded during the year. This figure is higher than in 2022 when Repo transactions accounted for 60.2% of the total traded.

The CDA market and the banking system vs. the capital market.

In the stock market, there are wider ranges to diversify rates than in the financial market. However, the stock market is still viewed with mistrust by the public. There is a large rate advantage gap:

- **CDAs:** According to reports from the Central Bank of Paraguay, in December 2023, the average bank interest rates for CDs with terms longer than 365 days were 8.43% in PYG and 6.17% in USD.
- **Traditional system or savings bank:** The report from the Central Bank notes that the approximate average rate for attracting money in demand deposits or bank savings accounts was 0.64% for foreign currency and 0.94% for local currency.
- **Stock market:** According to the BVA report, in 2023, the interest rate in the stock market for fixed-income operations in foreign currency or dollars was 5.83%, with an average term of 7.87 years. For fixed-income operations in guaranies, the average interest rate was 8.63% with an average term of 7.77 years.

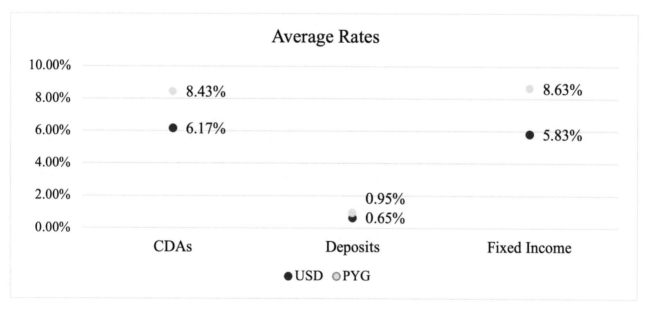

Average Interest Rates December 2023.
Source: Own elaboration with data from the Central Bank and the Asunción Stock Exchange.

Credit Rating Agencies.

In Paraguay, risk rating agencies are supervised by the National Securities Commission (CNV). Their exclusive purpose is the risk rating of banks and other financial entities, insurance companies, cooperatives, companies that issue debt securities and securities, shareholders, and in general, any security of public or private offering, representing debt or capital, investment fund shares, mutual fund shares.

In 1997, the first legal framework for the agencies' operations was established with Act No. 1056/97, which only mentioned the legal framework for qualifying securities offered publicly or privately. It also noted a series of requirements for agency operation in the country (minimum capital, legal form, etc.). Due to the narrow local market and other conjunctural factors, they became barriers to the effective establishment of rating agencies in Paraguay.

In 2009, after modifying the legal framework prepared by the CNV, a new Act No. 3899 was enacted, which regulates Risk Rating Companies and repealed the previous Act (1056/97). Included among the most important changes introduced were the extension of the rating obligation to other entities of the financial system and the withdrawal of the minimum capital required for establishing foreign agencies.

Rating Categories.

Debt securities are divided according to short-term (maturity up to 365 days), medium (maturity between 366 and 1095 days), and long-term (maturity greater than 1095 days). Short-term securities will be classified in levels ranging from "N-1 to N-5", where:

The rating categories for public offering securities are established in CNV Resolution No. 1241/09, where the prefix "py" will be prepended to distinguish that it is a rating on a national scale.

- **Level 1 (N-1):** The highest capacity to pay principal and interest in the agreed terms and terms. It would not be affected by possible changes in the issuer, industry, or economy.
- **Level 2 (N-2):** Good capacity to pay principal and interest in the agreed terms and terms but is susceptible to deterioration in the event of possible changes in the issuer, in the industry, or the economy.
- **Level 3 (N-3):** Sufficient capacity to pay principal and interest in the agreed terms and terms, but it is susceptible to weakening due to possible changes in the issuer, industry, or economy.
- **Level 4 (N-4):** The ability to pay principal and interest in agreed terms and terms does not meet the requirements to qualify at levels N-1, N-2, N-3.
- **Level 5 (N-5):** Corresponds to those instruments whose issuer does not have representative information for the minimum period required for the rating, and there are not sufficient guarantees.

The medium and long term are classified with letters ranging from "AAA to E." For the latter, trend indicators (+), (-), or observations may be incorporated to show relative positions within the rating categories from "AA to B," where:

- **Category AAA:** Instruments with the highest capacity to pay principal and interest in the agreed terms and terms, which would not be affected by changes in the issuer, industry, or economy.
- **Category AA:** Instruments with a very high capacity to pay principal and interest in the agreed terms and terms, which would not be significantly affected by possible changes in the issuer, industry, or economy.
- **Category A:** Instruments with a good capacity to pay principal and interest in the agreed terms and terms that are susceptible to slight deterioration due to possible changes in the issuer, industry, or economy.
- **BBB Category:** Instruments with sufficient capacity to pay principal and interest in the agreed terms and terms that are susceptible to weakening due to possible changes in the issuer, industry, or economy.
- **Category BB:** Instruments with the ability to pay capital and interest in agreed terms and terms that are susceptible to deterioration due to possible changes in the issuer, industry, or economy and may incur a delay in the payment of interest and/or capital.
- **Category B:** Instruments that have the minimum capacity to pay capital and interest in the agreed terms and terms that are susceptible to deterioration due to possible changes in the issuer, industry, or economy and which may incur a loss of interest and capital.
- **Category C:** Instruments that do not have sufficient payment capacity for the payment of capital and interest in agreed terms and terms, with a high risk of loss of capital and interest or a requirement to call creditors in progress.
- **Category D:** Instruments without the capacity to pay principal and interest in the agreed terms and terms that present an effective default of payment of interest or principal or a bankruptcy requirement in progress.
- **Category E:** Instruments whose issuer has insufficient information or does not have representative information for the minimum period required for the rating, and there are insufficient guarantees.

The rating category for stocks ranges from "Category I to Category VI," thus being:

- **Category I:** The highest level of solvency with very good profit-generating capacity.
- **Category II:** High level of solvency and good capacity to generate profits.
- **Category III:** Good level of solvency and acceptable capacity to generate profits.
- **Category IV:** Solvency slightly lower than Category III and weak profit-generating capacity.
- **Category V:** Weak solvency situation and uncertain profit-generating capacity.
- **Category VI:** Stock certificates whose issuer does not have representative information for the minimum period required for the rating, that is, without sufficient information.

For equity fund shares, the rating categories are classified into first class and second-class shares without sufficient information in view of the investment policy of the fund, the expected loss due to non-payment of the securities in which it invests, market risk, the management capacity of the management company and other risk factors or elements determined at the discretion of the rating agency.

And, for those instrument ratings not referred to in the previous sections, the Rating Agencies will use their own scales and definitions. They must report them to the commission for approval.

The risk rating agencies registered and authorized before the National Securities Commission (CNV) to operate in Paraguay are:

- Solventa S.A. - Registered and authorized according to CNV Res. No.: 1251/10.
- Feller Rate - Registered and enabled according to CNV Res. No.: 1279/10.
- Evaluadora Latinoamericana S.A. - Registered and authorized according to CNV Res. No.: 1290/10.
- Riskmetrica S.A. - Registered and authorized according to CNV Res. No.: 7E / 16.
- FIX SCR S.A. - Registered and authorized according to CNV Res. No.: 1E / 16.

C H A P T E R

III

Bi Monetarism, Saving Mechanisms and Derivative Instruments

Paraguay is an attractive market for investment, as it has a stable macroeconomy and low taxes. It is also an excellent platform for operating in other South American countries. Its economy is predictable, with controlled inflation levels. Despite being a developing country, Paraguay has achieved investment-grade status, which reinforces its stability and confidence in the international market. However, it is still necessary to address some of its deficiencies to enhance its competitiveness and attract more investments.

A strong macroeconomic environment and monetary stability are the foundation of Paraguay's success, which is a stark contrast to most of its neighbors. Macroeconomics does not solve all its problems, but it does ensure a relatively calm and predictable business environment, with a local currency used for many daily transactions and savings.

Paraguay has shown significant progress in its credit rating over the past few years. In July 2024, Moody's upgraded the country's sovereign rating to Baa3 with a stable outlook, achieving the much-anticipated investment grade. This change reflects confidence in Paraguay's economic stability and its ability to manage external shocks. Similarly, in February 2024, Standard & Poor's (S&P) upgraded the country's rating from BB to BB+, also with a stable outlook. Meanwhile, Fitch maintained Paraguay's rating at BB+, likewise with a stable outlook. As of September 2024, the rating agency was conducting its annual review.

Brief Notes on the Paraguay Economy

Paraguay stands as the fastest-growing economy in terms of GDP. By the end of the first quarter of 2024, according to the National Accounts report from the Central Bank of Paraguay (BCP), the economy grew by 4.3%, making it the country with the highest GDP expansion in the region. In contrast, neighboring countries Argentina and Brazil recorded changes of -5.1% and 2.5%, respectively.

At the end of the first semester, the Monthly Economic Activity Indicator (IMAEP) recorded an accumulated variation of 4.4%. For 2024, the Central Bank of Paraguay (BCP) estimates that GDP will grow by 3.8%, indicating an expected slowdown in the growth rate during the second semester.

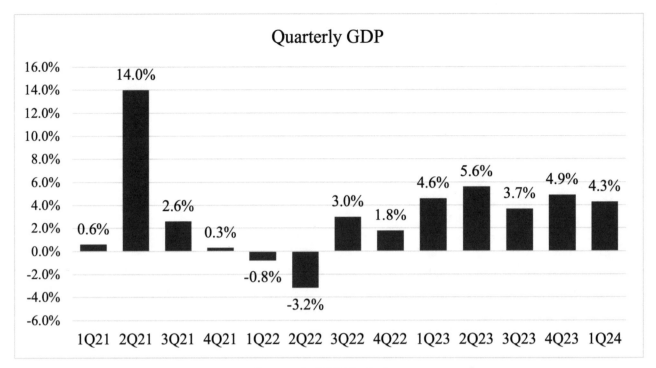

Quarterly GDP Variation.
Source: Statistical Annex Central Bank of Paraguay August 2024.

However, Paraguay's GDP per capita is significantly lower than that of its neighbors. During the 2020 pandemic, the GDP per capita fell to $4,984 from $5,419 in 2019. It has gradually recovered, reaching $5,693 in 2023, and is expected to rise to $5,906 in 2024. In contrast, Argentina's GDP per capita is $12,625 (2023) and Brazil's is $9,032 (2023).

According to official data, Paraguay has the lowest level of public debt in the region. After the pandemic, public debt grew steadily. In 2019, according to the Public Debt Statistics from the Ministry of Economy, it represented 22.9% of GDP, which amounted to US$ 8.859 billion. During the 2020 pandemic, this figure climbed to 33.8% of GDP, or about US$ 12.213 billion. Much of this increase is due to strategies implemented to help mitigate the pandemic's impact and to stimulate economic recovery. By 2023, public debt closed at US$ 16.566 billion, representing 38.5% of GDP. Although this figure is rising, it remains significantly lower than Argentina's 91.1% and Brazil's 74.3%.

Unemployment and informality and poverty

However healthy the formal economy is, consideration should be given to the informal economy to understand money flows and real GDP. Although a serious analysis of the informal economy largely exceeds the focus of this work, some consideration should be given to it because of its magnitude and relative influence in the financial sector and capital markets.

According to data from the National Institute of Statistics, at the end of 2023, the total number of people employed was 2,372,030, of which 54.75% were men and 45.25% were women. Additionally, the proportion of people employed in an occupation classified as informal was 62.1% for that same year. In absolute terms, this affected around 1,472,704 people, of which 59.7% were men and 65.0% were women.

It is also notable that despite Paraguay being a rich country, it has a large segment of the population living in extreme poverty. This, at least according to the authors of this article, is an indicator of potential social unrest that could lead to policies driven by socialist voters and changes in the structure of fiscal income and external debt, a trend already seen and widespread in South America. According to data published by the National Institute of Statistics regarding the total population in 2023 (5,871,814), 1,330,892 people are in poverty, and another 289,641 people are in extreme poverty.

Total poverty in Paraguay decreased by 2.8 percentage points in 2023, dropping from 25.5% (2022) to 22.7% (2023). On the other hand, extreme poverty decreased by 1.2 percentage points, from 6.1% (2022) to 4.9% (2023). This economic condition affects the rural area (207,171 people) more than the urban area (82,470 people). The government explained that the reduction in extreme poverty rates was due to the implementation of social aid programs.

The Guaraní is a stable currency that is used to save and invest.

The *Guaraní* has been the currency of legal tender in Paraguay since 1943. One of the oldest currencies in Latin America, it has not subtracted zeros nor undergone a change to its value since its creation. In January 2000, the value of the Gs. vs. $ was Gs.3,365. Since this date, the Guaraní has depreciated 105%, positioning its value in January 2024 at Gs. 7,286.68.

Saving and Investing in Paraguay

With a currency more stable than many of its South American peers, Paraguay's investment instruments are largely used by institutional and individual investors alike, roughly 50% in Gs and 50% in $. The most common financial instruments are Certificates of Deposit (CDs), with approximately $8 billion in circulation at the end of 2023, followed by various types of Government Bonds (federal, municipal, agency) traded in 2023 with a total value of $1.5 billion, and the corporate fixed-income market valued at US$ 3.2 billion, according to data from the Superintendency of Securities.

CDAs -similar to the American CDs but still issued in physical form- are plain vanilla time deposits that are issued by banks and financial institutions (*financieras*) and are regulated by the Central Bank, while PYG-denominated government and corporate bonds are traded on the Stock Exchange, generally through brokerage houses, and are regulated by the Superintendency of Securities.

Brief introduction to CDAs and Local PYG Bonds

CDA Market

CDAs, or term certificates of deposit, are issued by financial institutions and are partially guaranteed by the Deposit Guarantee Fund or 'FGD' (regulated by the Central Bank as provided in Law N° 2334) that in Article one subsection g mentioned the guarantee worth up to 75 minimum wages, equivalent to approximately $28,800 per person, regardless of the number of CDAs they have. There is an important secondary market trading in CDAs. Also, as the CDA is a bank deposit, an investor can ask the issuer bank to redeem the CDA at a negotiated discount.

Interest on CDAs is also negotiable. There is some available data, but it is not a set standard. It is not uncommon for financial institutions to issue CDAs on very different terms, depending on the investor and the bank issuer's own financing needs at that moment. Brokerage houses trade them OTC, as there is no screen or public information on the secondary market. The Central Bank offers some reference pricing, normally within a month. There have been several projects aimed at dematerializing, streamlining, standardizing, and publishing CDA information for the general public. However, to date, a standardized system that would allow for greater transparency and accessibility of the information has yet to be implemented. CDAs are still issued in physical form, either bearer or endorsable.

The President of the Superintendency of Securities, Joshua Abreu, expressed the entity's willingness and interest in digitalizing this instrument, projecting that it would be fully implemented by 2021. However, in 2023, the Central Bank of Paraguay issued a tender for the acquisition of the system for the dematerialization of CDAs, but the call for bids was unsuccessful.

In general terms, the interest rates in local currency offered in the CDs in December 2023 were 4.49% for a duration of 180 days or less, 6.84% for terms of 180 to 365 days, and 8.43% for terms longer than 365 days.

The minimum amount to issue a CDA in guaraníes varies according to each institution. On average, the minimum is Gs 1,000,000, equivalent to about $145.

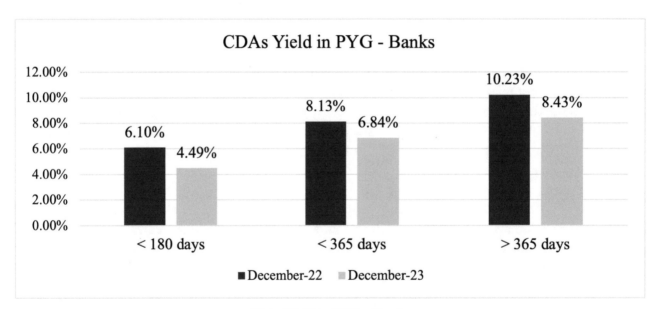

CDAs Yield in PYG – Banks.
Source: BCP Weighted Average Interest Rate Report December 2023.

The highest average yield recorded in the last thirteen years dates back to May 2011, with a rate of 10.80%. Since then, average rates have fluctuated significantly, with the lowest yield recorded in May 2021, with an average rate of 4.47%. In 2023, the weighted average yield ranged between a minimum of 7.82% and a maximum of 9.58%. The following graph shows the historical behavior of the weighted average deposit rates of the CDA in guaraníes over the last thirteen years.

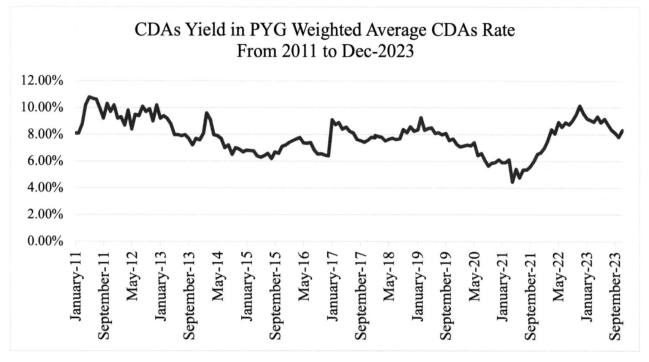

Weighted Average CDAs Rate – PYG.
Source: Own preparation with data from Financial Indicator December 2023.

In 2019, bank CDAs in guaraníes registered at the end of December a total deposit of $3,133.07 million (Gs. 21.6 trillion), 30% higher than that registered at the end of December 2018 ($2,408 million or Gs. 16.6 trillion). For 2020, a total of $3,227 million (Gs. 22.2 trillion) is registered. The value of the CDA portfolio as of December 2021 is $3,616 million (Gs. 24.9 trillion), equivalent to a growth of 12% compared to the end of 2020, according to data published by the BCP in its Statistical Annex of the Economic Report[16]. While at the end of 2023, the value of this portfolio was around $4,215 million, 15% higher compared to the values of 2022 ($3.866 million or Gs. 26.6 trillion).

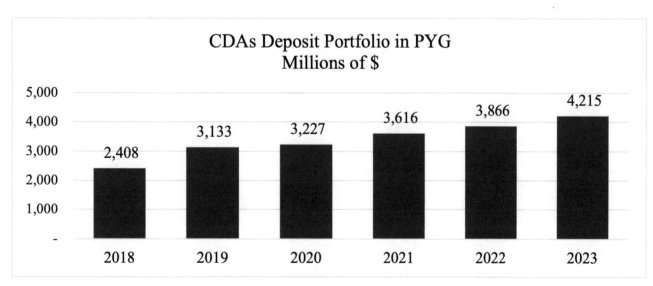

CDA deposit portfolio in PYG – Banks.
Source: BCP Superintendency Statical Bulletin - December 2023.

---

[16] https://www.bcp.gov.py/boletines-estadisticos-i62

Local currency CDs (Certificates of Deposit) hold a 38.2% share of the Guarani deposit market compared to other instruments such as Savings Accounts, Checking Accounts, and Fixed-Term Savings. In this context, the total volume of the Guarani deposit portfolio at the end of December 2023 was $11,028 million (Gs. 80.2 trillion), comprised of 38.2% in CDs, 32% in demand deposits, followed by 28.2% in Checking Accounts and 0.6% in Fixed-Term Savings.

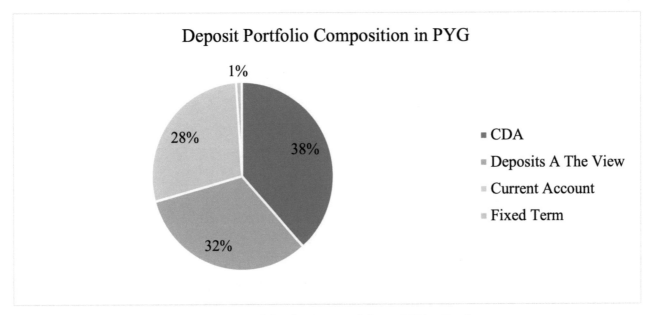

Composition of the deposit portfolio in PYG – Banks.
Source: BCP Superintendency Statistical Bulletin December 2023.

Guaraní Denominated Bond Market

Bonds denominated in PYG play a fundamental role in the Asunción Stock Exchange. By the end of 2023, bonds in Guarani accounted for approximately 65% of all market trades. The following chart shows the evolution of the share of trades in PYG.

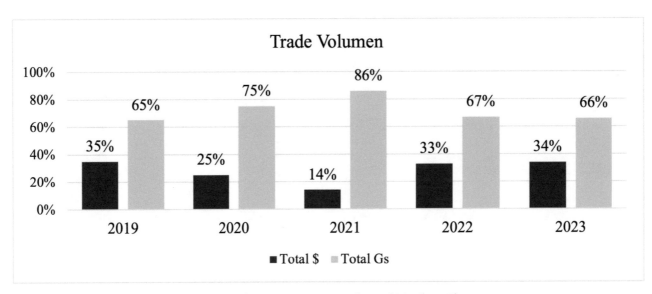

Evolution of PYG-Denominated Bond Trading Share.
Source: Superintendency of Securities.

In 2023, the Republic of Paraguay auctioned bonds in the market for a total value of USD 344 million, more compared to what was auctioned in 2022 (USD 7.6 million). The following chart shows the history of Treasury bonds denominated in PYG auctioned in the local market. We observe the progressive increase due to changes in policy, market appetite, and the social plan implemented during the COVID-19 pandemic.

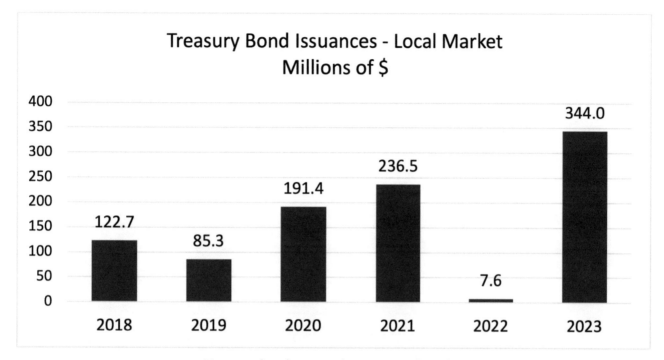

Treasury bond auction history. Local market.
Source: Outstanding bonds Ministry of Finance.

At the end of 2023, the Treasury's debt circulating in the local market amounts to $979 million (Gs. 6.85 billion), which represents 6% of the total public debt and 2% of GDP.

In the domestic market, securities are issued through the Central Bank of Paraguay and the Asunción Stock Exchange, with maturities currently ranging from 5 to 20 years. Part of the dynamism that the market experienced is due to the measures implemented between 2019 and 2021 by the Ministry of Economy, the Central Bank of Paraguay, and the Asunción Stock Exchange that contributed to facilitating the functioning of the Treasury market. The main measures consisted of the following:

- Implementation of the dematerialization of bonds as a replacement for paper instruments.
- Decree No. 3195/2015 of the general framework for the issuance, negotiation, placement, maintenance in circulation, and early redemption of General Treasury bonds.
- Formation of a Bond Placement Committee made up of representatives of the Treasury and BVA, with the power to evaluate the offers received through the exchange and accept or reject them according to technical criteria.
- Establishment of an advisory team, made up of representatives of the Ministry of Finance and the Central Bank of Paraguay, which is in charge of analyzing macroeconomic and market conditions, among other functions.
- Pre-announced annual auction calendar.
- Allowing the reopening of previously issued bond series.

- Periodic surveys among banks, the main investors in Treasury Securities, to update the market perspectives regarding terms and issuance rates.
- Standardization of interest and principal settlement processes and auction processes (through a Dutch auction).

As a result of these transformations, Paraguay has managed to improve the structure of the PYG-denominated Treasury market, obtaining financing for investments at attractive rates and picking up in terms of volumes and variety of offerings in the local market.

Regarding the corporate and municipal sector, in the local bond market denominated in Guarani, as of December 2023, around 35 companies issued debt securities for a total value of $490 million (Gs. 3.5 trillion).

After analyzing the data published by the BVA as of December 2023, the summary of rates and terms in Guarani, broken down by economic sector, is as follows:

Sector	Average Weighted Rate (%)	Term Average Weighted (Years)
Public	8.13%	8.84
Services	8.21%	7.57
Financial	8.28%	4.59
Commercial	10.89%	5.00
Construction	9.49%	9.94
Industrial	8.07%	6.14
Chemical	12.56%	4.07
Technology	11.70%	4.70
Agricultural	11.47%	4.51
Real Estate	11.43%	4.03

Weighted average rates and terms by economic sector. Local market.
Source: BVA Monthly Report 2023.

The US dollar is a common currency in Paraguay and is also used to save and invest.

Paraguay abandoned the Gold Standard in 1943, creating the guarani (Gs.) and, in a way, incorporating the US dollar into its daily practice. Between 1960 and 1985, the guaraní was pegged to the United States dollar. Today, roughly half the currency circulation and bank deposits are in $. Likewise, Paraguay Central Bank Reserves are held in $, Treasury international bonds are exclusively $ denominated, and exports of energy and agricultural commodities are also dollarized. Anecdotally, transactions of large capital assets (land, real estate, cars, trucks and tractors, machinery, and equipment) are priced and transacted in the American Dollar.

It's no wonder, then, that savers and investors are looking for $-denominated checking and savings accounts and CDAs, as well as locally issued bonds and occasionally $-denominated stocks.

According to the Financial Indicators reports published by the Central Bank, dollar deposits collected by Paraguayan banks maintained a strong growth dynamic throughout 2023, closing the year with a 12% increase compared to 2022, rising from $8,203 million to $9,195 million.

A Brief Introduction to CDAs and Bonds in US Dollars

The Certificates of Deposit (CDA) in dollars have shown steady growth over the past few years. In 2019, they reached $2,897 million (Gs. 19.9 trillion), 24% higher than the total for 2018 ($2,334 million or Gs. 16 trillion). However, in 2020, a slight decrease was recorded, with a total of $2,782 million (Gs. 19.1 trillion), representing a 4% drop compared to 2019. In 2021, the portfolio decreased again, standing at $2,744 million (Gs. 18.8 trillion). Nonetheless, in both 2022 and 2023, CDAs experienced significant increases of 18% and 17%, respectively.

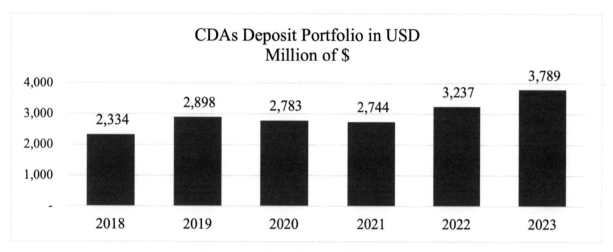

CDA deposit portfolio in PYG - Banks.
Source: BCP Superintendency Statistical Bulletin December 2023.

Following the analysis of the data published by the BCP, as of December 2023, the total volume of the deposit in dollars in the financial system reached $9,195 million (Gs. 57.9 trillion). This includes deposits of CDAs, deposits in current accounts, deposits A the View (unlike checking accounts, deposits A the View pay a small amount of interest for the money deposited) and Fixed Term.

CDA deposits occupy 41% of the portfolio, followed by deposits in A the View with 31% and checking account deposits with 25%. Fixed Term deposits occupy 2%. Once again, these figures confirm that CDAs are one of the preferred savings instruments. However, the data indicate that the highest deposits in CDA are in guaraníes.

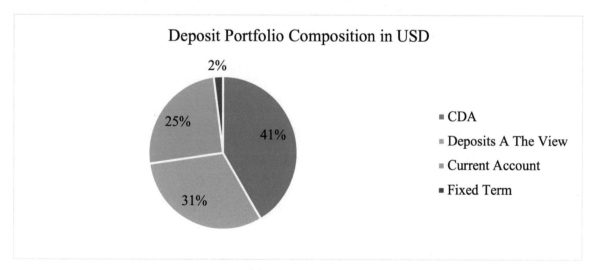

Deposit portfolio composition in $ – Banks.
Source: BCP Superintendency Statistical Bulletin December 2023.

On the other hand, the Central Bank of Paraguay reported the weighted average interest rates at the end of 2023. CDs in U.S. dollars recorded a yield of 4.31% for terms shorter than 180 days, 4.92% for terms between 180 and 365 days, and 6.17% for terms longer than 365 days.

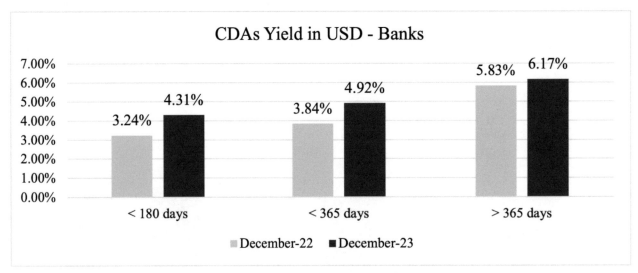

Yield CDAs in $ - Banks.
Source: BCP Weighted Average Interest Rate Report December 2023.

The following graph shows the historical behavior of CDA deposit rates in US dollars at the end of December 2023:

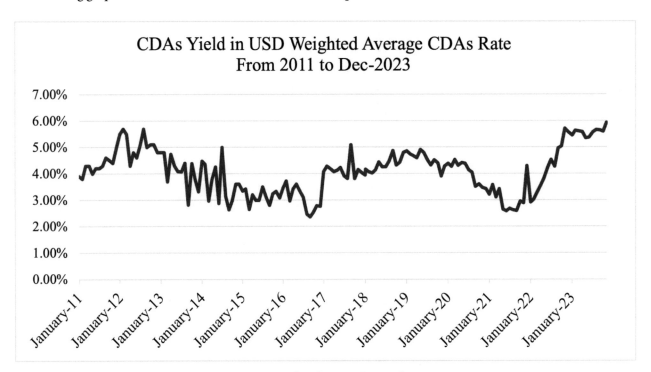

Source: Financial Indicator December 2023.

Total CDA Market

Concluding the analysis of the CDA market, the total in CDA deposits (including deposits in Gs and $) at the end of December 2023 was $8,003 million or Gs. 58 trillion. This figure represents 40% of the total deposit portfolio of $20,223 million or Gs. 147 trillion.

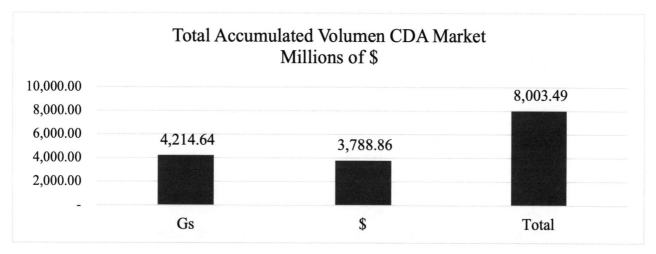

Source: BCP Superintendency Statistical Bulletin December 2023.

Of the total deposits in CDAs, five banks occupy more than 50% of the portfolio. The following is the ranking of banks in the CDA portfolio:

Entity	$ Million	Market Share %
Sudameris Bank S.A.E.C.A.	1.657,27	20.71%
Banco Continental S.A.E.C.A.	1.283,32	16.03%
Banco GNB Paraguay S.A.E.C.A.	943,17	11.78%
Banco Nacional de Fomento	744,83	9.31%
Banco Itaú Paraguay S.A.	498,99	6.23%
Banco BASA S.A.	492,34	6.15%
Banco Río S.A.E.C.A.	365,35	4.56%
Banco Atlas S.A.	347,21	4.34%
Visión Banco S.A.E.C.A.	345,81	4.32%
Banco Familiar S.A.E.C.A.	331,46	4.14%
Bancop S.A.	299,13	3.74%
Ueno Bank S.A.	223,40	2.79%
Interfisa Banco S.A.E.C.A.	214,50	2.68%
Solar Banco S.A.E	137,72	1.72%
Banco Do Brasil S.A.	101,92	1.27%
Banco de la Nación Argentina	17,06	0.21%
Citibank N.A.	0,00	0.00%
Total	**8.003,49**	

Source: BCP Superintendency Statistical Bulletin December 2023.

Introduction to US Dollar Bonds

As mentioned previously, Paraguay is a bi-monetary country, and dollar savings in different forms has been the norm for more than half a century. In addition, the country is gradually gaining a place in international markets, receiving foreign investment in dollars.

Historically, Paraguay's financing depended on loans from multilateral, bilateral, and commercial banks. Paraguay's largest creditors were the Inter-American Development Bank (IDB) and the Development Bank of Latin America and the Caribbean (CAF).

These loans were mainly used to finance infrastructure and social development programs. However, despite having a low average financing cost, the concentration of financing with multilateral and bilateral organizations limited the government's ability to respond quickly to investment needs due to the bureaucratic processes involved in negotiations of this type.

Paraguay's debut in the international market in 2013, with the issuance of a bond worth 500 million dollars for a 10-year term and a yield rate of 4.625%, marks Paraguay's return to international capital markets since the 19th century. The inaugural interest rate for a sovereign bond debut was the lowest in the history of Latin American financial markets. Paraguay has continued to approach international markets in the last decade with new issuances, reaching a total placement of $7.186 million by the end of 2023, which represents 40% of total public debt and 17% of GDP. See details in the table below:

	Issue Date	Maturity Date	Amount (US$)	Nominal Rate (%)	Duration (Years)
Sovereign Bond 23	25/1/13	25/1/23	780,000,000	4.625	10
Sovereign Bond 2044	11/8/14	11/8/44	1,000,000,000	6.10	30
Sovereign Bond 2026	23/3/16	15/4/26	600,000,000	5,00	10
Sovereign Bond 2027	22/3/17	27/3/27	500,000,000	4.70	10
Sovereign Bond 2048	8/3/18	13/3/48	530,000,000	5.60	30
Sovereign Bond 2050	4/2/19	30/3/50	1,175,858,000	5.40	31
Sovereign Bond 2031	23/4/20	28/4/31	1,000,000,000	4.95	11
Sovereign Bond 2033	20/1/21	29/1/33	600,000,000	2.739	11
Sovereign Bond 2033_2	20/1/22	28/6/33	500,600,000	3.849	10
Sovereign Bond 2033_3	28/6/23	21/8/33	500,000,000	5.850	10

Paraguay Sovereign Bonds.
Source: Own elaboration with data from the Ministry of Economy.

In 2015, the reopening of the 2023 Bond was carried out for a value of $280 million at a cutoff rate of 4.15%. In 2020, a reopening of the 2050 Bond was carried out for a value of $450 million at a cutoff rate of 4.45%. In 2021, the reopening of the 2050 Bond was carried out for a value of $225.8 million at a cutoff rate of 4.089%, along with a buyback of the 2023 Bond for $329.506 million. In 2022, the buyback of the 2023 Bond was carried out for $212.9 million and of the 2026 Bond for $72.9 million. In 2023, a buyback of the 2026 Bond was carried out for $70.264 million.

It is worth mentioning that in 2021, even during the COVID-19 pandemic, the successful issuance of sovereign bonds on the international market stood out, amounting to $600 million with an interest rate of 2.74%, the lowest in the history of Paraguay's bond issuances. Additionally, through Law No. 6638 on liability management, which authorizes the Executive Branch, through the Ministry of Economy, to manage previously issued debts and renegotiate the respective interest rates, a bond buyback was achieved.

Regarding the U.S. dollar bond market for the private or corporate sector, the traded volume is much lower than that of bonds in guaraníes. Data from the Asunción Stock Exchange indicates that the corporate and municipal sector debt in the local dollar bond market in 2023 was US$ 116 million.

After analyzing the data published by the BVA as of December 2023, the summary of interest rates and terms in U.S. dollars, divided by economic sector, is as follows:

Sector	Average Weighted Rate (%)	Term Average Weighted (Years)
Financial	5.58%	8.07
Construction	5.73%	8.01
Commercial	6.40%	6.61
Industrial	5.36%	9.97
Agriculture	7.76%	3.70
Services	7.26%	6.18
Technology	7.76%	4.04
Real Estate	9.10%	3.38

Source: BVA monthly reports.

The Paraguayan stock market has positioned itself as one of the most dynamic sectors, registering records in volumes traded year after year.

How many dollars are there in circulation?

Obtaining a precise number of U.S. dollars in circulation is quite difficult because the Central Bank does not act as a clearing agent. However, in general, we can get an indication by considering different variables, such as Paraguay's Net International Reserves (NIR), which, according to BCP publications as of December 2023, stood at around $10,196.8 million. This amount is 5% higher compared to $9,825 million in the same period of 2022.

Additionally, the total U.S. dollar deposits in the banking system as of December 2023, according to the statistical bulletin of the Central Bank of Paraguay, amounts to $9,195.26 million, which represents 45% of the total deposits system of $20,223.46 million (consolidating guaraníes and dollars).

In terms of the volume of foreign currency sales to the financial and public sectors, accumulated between January and December 2023, carried out by the Central Bank of Paraguay, a total of $1,129.58 million was recorded. As a result, the intervention carried out by the BCP was 19% lower than that recorded in the same month of the previous year ($1,406.82 million).

Who clears Guaraníes and Dollars?

In Paraguay, the Central Bank of Paraguay has authorized the Bancard S.A. company to administer the Check Clearing House from April 3, 2017, according to resolution No. 4 of the BCP, which authorizes said private company to operate as a banking clearinghouse, but only for checks. As it is legendary, Prosegur S.A., the largest operator of armored trucks, is considered the largest depositor of US dollar notes outside the banking system.

Active intervention policies of the Central Bank of Paraguay

After the financial crises of 1995 and 1998 and the comprehensive reordering of monetary and financial policy, fundamental laws for macroeconomic stabilization were enacted. On the one hand, Law No. 489/ of the Organic Charter of the Central Bank of Paraguay, where the central bank is assigned the responsibility and power to ensure the stability of the value of the currency and promote the effectiveness of the financial system, assigning functions, duties, and attributions to the authorities for the fulfillment of their objectives. On the other hand, General Law No. 861/96 of Banks, Finance Companies and Other Credit Institutions provided a much stricter regulatory framework than its predecessor.

As of the promulgation of these laws, the bank concentrated on achieving and maintaining low and stable inflation, implementing a monetary program framed in its objective.

In May 2011, the Central Bank of Paraguay decided to formally initiate the implementation of the inflation targeting scheme for the management of monetary policy, which was under Resolution No. 22 dated May 18, 2011, where it mentions that "The referred scheme, in addition to specifying quantitative inflation targets, implies transparency in the strategy and implementation of monetary policy to guide the expectations of economic agents, as well as the prospective evaluation of the pressures on the general price level, based on a wide variety of information. The scheme also corresponds to market mechanisms, through which the monetary policy interest rate affects key variables of the economy. The lower variability of inflation and its predictability are expected results of the new adopted scheme"[17].

Monetary Policy Rate

The Monetary Policy Rate (MPR) is the main instrument used by the Bank to achieve the inflation target. In practice, the MPR is a reference interest rate for determining the cost of money and other financial prices, such as the exchange rate and longer-term interest rates. In turn, these variables affect the demand for goods and services and, in this way, prices and inflation.

The main objective of the Central Bank of Paraguay is to ensure the stability of the guaraní. The implementation of the monetary policy rate (TPM) began in 2011, and since then, the rates have generally trended downward. The average rate from its inception until February 2020 was 5.56%. In response to the COVID-19 pandemic in March 2020, the BCP significantly reduced the TPM from 4% to a historic low of 0.75%. In 2021, due to rising inflationary pressures, particularly in the second half of the year, the BCP initiated an upward adjustment of the TPM, raising it from 0.75% to 5.25% by December 2021. Throughout 2022, the TPM continued

---

[17] Texto extraído de: https://repositorio.bcp.gov.py/bitstream/handle/123456789/159/Manual_Metas%20de%20inflación%20un%20nuevo%20esquema.pdf?sequence=1&isAllowed=y

to rise, ending the year at 8.50%. However, in 2023, the Central Bank implemented several rate cuts, lowering the reference rate to 6.75% by December.

Inflation Targeting

In 2004, the BCP began to make efforts to adopt inflation targets. Finally, in May 2011, the BCP officially announced the implementation of a new regime in the conduct of monetary policy called Inflation Goals (MI). With this scheme, the monetary authority sets an explicit numerical inflation target and thereby assumes the commitment to meet it through proper monetary policy management.

Initially, the goal was set at 5% per year and a tolerance range of +/- 2.5%. This meant inflation could fluctuate between 2.5% and 7.5%. In 2014, the range of goals decreased to +/- 2.0%. A year later, the inflationary goal decreased to 4.5%, and it finally remained at 4% as of 2017, maintaining that objective to this day.

According to the report from the Central Bank of Paraguay, the Paraguayan economy showed a notable improvement in inflation control during 2023. The accumulated inflation rate at the end of the year stood at 3.7%, a figure significantly lower than the 8.1% recorded in 2022. This figure coincides with the year-on-year inflation rate, also at 3.7%. In December, the monthly inflation was 0.3%. It is important to mention that these results fall within the target range established by the Central Bank of Paraguay.

Historical $/Gs rates

In December 2023, the Central Bank of Paraguay's wholesale reference price for US dollars closed at $/PYG 7,263.59 for buying and $/PYG 7,283.62 for selling. According to BCP records, the highest peak that year was reached on November 1st, when it stood at 7,474.57 PYG. The dollar appreciated 0.07% compared to January 2023 ($1 / PYG 7,269.13) and depreciated 0.24% compared to November 30 ($1 / PYG 7,419.12). The lowest price historically published by the Central Bank of Paraguay dates back to January 1997 with a price of $1 / PYG 2,128.

On the other hand, the RIN (Net International Reserves) that the BCP has to intervene in the market and face transitory difficulties in the balance of payments, maintain the normality of transactions in the free exchange market and preserve the external value of the currency as of December 2023, was $10,196.8 million.

According to historical data published by the BCP in its Statistical Annex, the worst moment recorded in the Paraguayan economy was in 2002. At that time, international reserves reached minimum values, reaching only about $571.2 million. With this, the price of the dollar rose, reaching over $1/Gs. 7,104. After almost 20 years, and because of the effects of the pandemic caused by COVID-19, in 2020, the price was close to reaching its historic highs, reaching $1/Gs. 7,032 in November of that year.

Currency hedge mechanisms in the local market

$/Gs futures and forwards with banks market and in BVA.

Bank Forward Contracts

Forwards are bilateral contracts between two banks or a bank and customer setting the purchase or sale of a $ or Gs. in a relatively short future, agreeing on the exchange rate on the purchase date. Most contracts are concentrated in the 90 to 360-day range. Very unusually, contracts can be for a longer duration. The BCP regulation establishes that the term of a currency forward operation may not exceed 36 months. The contracts are not negotiable in a secondary market, and furthermore, they cannot be canceled unilaterally.

According to reports published by the BCP, the volume of forward operations of the financial system for purchases from January to July 2021 was $529.89 million, with terms ranging between three and 527 days. On the sales side, the volume is around $909.17 million, with terms ranging between eight and 399 days.

As in most markets, there are two forms of forward: delivery or 'Full Delivery Forward,' where the parties are obliged to deliver the currencies that are the object of the operation. The modality without delivery, or 'Non-delivery Forward,' consists of an operation in which compliance is given through the settlement of differences (compensation mechanism) and without underlying physical delivery.

The forward is an instrument aimed at corporations, companies, and financial institutions. The closing of operations is carried out by telephone or authorized electronic means.

The Central Bank of Paraguay regulates the currency forward through Board Resolution No. 8, dated February 2013, which approved the "Regulations for Forward Foreign Currency Purchase and Sale Operations (Foreign Currency Forward)."

Futures Contract at BVA

Futures contracts are agreements traded on the Product Exchange (formerly BVPASA), which is currently non-operational or on pause due to a lack of market demand. Futures contracts are standardized in terms of quantities, delivery dates, and prices, and are publicly known, with the Bolsa acting as the central counterparty that mitigates the risk of default by the intervening parties. To guarantee delivery, the BVA requires margins on contracts as needed.

BVA contracts have four available tenors, that is, 4-month futures quotes. This serves, for example, so that merchants who need to make purchases in dollars in those months can acquire a currency futures contract, which will allow them to manage their exchange rate on the date that they need to pay off their debt.

How are the instruments reflected in the market? Is there more of one than the other?

Currently, the interbank currency forward market is much larger than the BVA futures market. In addition, despite its advantages with the guarantee and dispute resolution mechanism, foreign exchange futures contracts have the lowest trading volume. There is a lack of knowledge and stock market education for the public and companies who are still familiar with locking currency obligations with banks. There is no speculative activity in this particular instrument either.

Printed in the United States
by Baker & Taylor Publisher Services